Early American Politics
By Kimmy Darlene Gerred

1. Keene, Cornell, O'Donnell "The Whig Vision Of Politics" Visions Of America 2nd Editions pg. 60 (2013)

ANGLO-AMERICAN POLITICS
THE WHIGS VS. THE TORIES; THE PEOPLE'S
PARLIAMENT VS. MONARCHY

1. Keene, Cornell, O'Donnell "The Whig Vision Of Politics" Visions Of America 2nd Editions pg. 60 (2013)

Kimmy Gerred

March 22, 2015

1. Keene, Cornell, O'Donnell "The Whig Vision Of
Politics" Visions Of America 2nd Editions
pg. 60 (2013)

ANGLO-AMERICAN POLITICS
THE WHIGS VS. THE TORIES; THE PEOPLE'S PARLIAMENT VS. MONARCHY

Virginia House of Burgesses 1619

One of the first political actions that happened in the United States happened in Virginia's new legislative body when the House of Burgesses (representatives) first convened in July 1619. (Visions of America pg. 39).

House of Burgesses Virginia, 1619

1. Keene, Cornell, O'Donnell "The Whig Vision Of Politics" Visions Of America 2nd Editions pg. 60 (2013)

House of Burgesses
Virginia 1619

Lord Baltimore's Proprietor Of Maryland

1. Keene, Cornell, O'Donnell "The Whig Vision Of Politics" Visions Of America 2nd Editions pg. 60 (2013)

James I died in 1625 which placed his son Charles I on the throne 1625-1649. He had married French Princess who was Catholic named Henrietta. Most of England was protestant.

But George Calvert, Lord Baltimore was Catholic and wanted to partake in the wealth of Americas so he obtained a royal charter for land in Virginia.

George Calvert died in 1632. His son Cecil requested a royal charter for a colony from King Charles. Maryland became the haven for English Catholics under the authority of Lord Baltimore.

1. Keene, Cornell, O'Donnell "The Whig Vision Of Politics" Visions Of America 2nd Editions pg. 60 (2013)

Cecil Calvert
Lord Baltimore's Son

1. Keene, Cornell, O'Donnell "The Whig Vision Of
Politics" Visions Of America 2nd Editions
pg. 60 (2013)

The Mayflower Compact 1620

The second political movement in the U.S was when William Bradford and the Mayflower landed off the coast of Cape Cod in a place that is now known to be Massachusetts in the fall of 1620.

Realizing they were not in Virginia as they had planned they drew up a set of binding laws and principals that would govern their settlement and community known as the "Mayflower Compact 1620".

The signers did "solemnly and mutually, in the Presence of God and on another, covenant and combine together into a civil body Politick, for our better Ordering and Preservation, and Furtherance of the Ends aforesaid" (Visions of America pg. 44).

1. Keene, Cornell, O'Donnell "The Whig Vision Of Politics" Visions Of America 2nd Editions pg. 60 (2013)

The Mayflower Signers
Cape Cod 1620

1. Keene, Cornell, O'Donnell "The Whig Vision Of Politics" Visions Of America 2nd Editions pg. 60 (2013)

The Mayflower Compact 1620

Mayflower Signers Original
Cape Cod 1620

1. Keene, Cornell, O'Donnell "The Whig Vision Of Politics" Visions Of America 2nd Editions pg. 60 (2013)

The Mayflower Compact 1620

IN THE NAME OF GOD, AMEN We, whose names are under-
written, the Loyal Subjects of our dread Sovereign Lord King James,
by the Grace of God, of Great Britain, France, and Ireland, King,
Defender of the Faith, &c. Having undertaken for the Glory of God,
and Advancement of the Christian Faith, and the Honour of our
King and Country, a Voyage to plant the first Colony in the northern Parts of Virginia; Do by these Presents, solemnly and mutually,
in the Presence of God and one another, covenant and combine our-
selves together into a civil Body Politick, for our better Ordering and
Preservation, and Furtherance of the Ends aforesaid: And by Virtue
hereof do enact, constitute, and frame, such just and equal Laws,
Ordinances, Acts, Constitutions, and Officers, from time to time, as
shall be thought most meet and convenient for the general Good of
the Colony; unto which we promise all due Submission and Obedience.

IN WITNESS whereof we have hereunto subscribed our names at
Cape-Cod the eleventh of November, in the Reign of our Sovereign
Lord King James, of England, France, and Ireland, the eighteenth, and
of Scotland the fifty-fourth, Anno Domini, 1620.

1. Keene, Cornell, O'Donnell "The Whig Vision Of
Politics" Visions Of America 2nd Editions
pg. 60 (2013)

Catholic Monarchy King Charles I Later Executed

Meanwhile, across the great Atlantic, the vast and furious sea in 1629 King Charles I vowed to dissolve the Parliament and he continued to restore elements of the Catholic ritual to the English Church.

King Charles I Monarchy

1. Keene, Cornell, O'Donnell "The Whig Vision Of Politics" Visions Of America 2nd Editions pg. 60 (2013)

Puritan John Winthrop and Massachusetts

A year later a Puritan John Winthrop brought a group of Puritans to New England to pursue their protestant faith. By 1630 twenty thousand (20,000) Puritans left England for New England. Winthrop became the first governor of Massachusetts.

John Winthrop Massechussetts 1st Governor

1. Keene, Cornell, O'Donnell "The Whig Vision Of Politics" Visions Of America 2nd Editions pg. 60 (2013)

Separation of Church and State for Protection of Religious Liberties by Roger Williams 1635

In 1635 Roger Williams (a devout Separatist minister) attacked the Puritan Orthodoxy form of government that Puritan John Winthrop said "A family is a little common wealth and a common wealth is a great family." And there was a set of beliefs that were based on the fifth commandment "Honor thy father and thy mother." and sought to avoid folk traditions of culture. By 1650 many Christmas traditions were banned.

Puritan law also insisted on sobriety and banned Christmas. Roger Williams sought to prevent the government from controlling the church. While Winthrop sought to control the church through government with his Puritan Orthodoxy.

Winthrop respected Williams piety and intellect however Massachusetts Bay would not allow his challenge to the states authority to enforce religious orthodoxy. (Competing Visions: antinomianism or Toleration: The Puritan Dilemma. Pg. 47)

1. Keene, Cornell, O'Donnell "The Whig Vision Of Politics" Visions Of America 2nd Editions pg. 60 (2013)

Roger Williams Providence, 1635

1. Keene, Cornell, O'Donnell "The Whig Vision Of Politics" Visions Of America 2nd Editions pg. 60 (2013)

Providence Rhode Island: Religious Liberties Free From Government Control

William Rogers left Massachusetts and founded Providence, Rhode Island. In 1634 another challenge to Puritans teachings came along. A great speaker arose and this time it was a female. Anne Hutchinson claimed only one minister was preaching true Calvinist idea that God's grace alone brought salvation not man's good works.

Anne Hutchinson

1. Keene, Cornell, O'Donnell "The Whig Vision Of Politics" Visions Of America 2nd Editions pg. 60 (2013)

Anne Hutchinson 1634

1. Keene, Cornell, O'Donnell "The Whig Vision Of Politics" Visions Of America 2nd Editions pg. 60 (2013)

Anne Hutchinson: Saved By Grace and Not Of Works

The Massachusetts Bay leaders of the colony were afraid that Hutchinson's followers would become an Antinomian heresy. "Antinomians took the logic of Calvinism to the extreme that Grace need not follow any earthly laws. The Puritans feared that it would lead to moral anarchy."

Anne Hutchinson was tried in 1637 and convicted then banished from the colony. She moved to Long Island. Thankfully, the British Empire would help to resolve some of the ridiculousness going on in Massachusetts when the British Civil war began in 1642 when Parliament emerged and tried the kind for his crimes against the people.

1. Keene, Cornell, O'Donnell "The Whig Vision Of Politics" Visions Of America 2nd Editions pg. 60 (2013)

The Fall of The Catholic Monarchy

Oliver Cromwell assumed the title Lord Protector of England and raised an army against the king, lifted censorship and allowed freedom of the press for the first time in 1649 when they executed King Charles I. Parliament inaugurated a new policy of religious toleration for all Protestants. (Visions of America pg.48)

Oliver Cromwell 1649

1. Keene, Cornell, O'Donnell "The Whig Vision Of Politics" Visions Of America 2nd Editions pg. 60 (2013)

The Quakers

Next was the revival movement of the Quakers and George Fox. The Quakers were merely interested in God's word. They rejected the need for any ministry at all. They felt that anyone could preach if they felt the spark of the spirit move within them.

The Quakers

1. Keene, Cornell, O'Donnell "The Whig Vision Of Politics" Visions Of America 2nd Editions pg. 60 (2013)

The Quakers

1. Keene, Cornell, O'Donnell "The Whig Vision Of Politics" Visions Of America 2nd Editions pg. 60 (2013)

Thomas Hooker & The Connecticut Valley

The third political movement in the U.S. happened after Thomas Hooker took a group from Massachusetts to Hartford, Connecticut in 1638 when representatives from Connecticut drafted a frame of government (The Fundamental Orders of Connecticut).

This expansion into Connecticut Valley brought about a fight with the Pequot Indians who refused to submit to English authority.

New Englanders sided with enemy tribes of the Pequot Indians who were the Narragansett and Mohegan Indians and fought against the Pequot Indians. This tactic of the New Englanders terrified the other Indian tribes.

1. Keene, Cornell, O'Donnell "The Whig Vision Of Politics" Visions Of America 2nd Editions pg. 60 (2013)

Thomas Hooker

1. Keene, Cornell, O'Donnell "The Whig Vision Of
Politics" Visions Of America 2nd Editions
pg. 60 (2013)

The Dutch Fur Trade Envy of England

The British Empire wanted to regain control over the wealth from the fur trade that the Dutch had been accumulating in through Dutch merchant ships. King Charles II gave his brother James Duke of York a charter for the area to recapture the fur trade from the Dutch industry in New Netherland 1664.

The Dutch Governor of New Netherlands Peter Stuyvesant tried to gather a force against the English invasion but the Dutch merchants realized it would be wiser if they oblige the English forces rather than fight them.

The Fourth political movement occurred in New York after the division of the fur trade in the region happened giving the English the New York side and the Dutch the New Jersey side. James tried to take complete control over New York but the New Yorkers refused to pay taxes. James relented and the fourth political movement was when New York assembly convened in 1683.

1. Keene, Cornell, O'Donnell "The Whig Vision Of Politics" Visions Of America 2nd Editions pg. 60 (2013)

The Dutch Fur Traders

The Great Governor William Penn of
Pennsylvania: With A Heart for the Indians

1. Keene, Cornell, O'Donnell "The Whig Vision Of
Politics" Visions Of America 2nd Editions
pg. 60 (2013)

The fifth political move was when William Penn formulated a government based on a number or new ideas in English politics like the writing of The English political philosopher James Harrington who believed a stable society depended on broad distribution of property.

William Penn

1. Keene, Cornell, O'Donnell "The Whig Vision Of Politics" Visions Of America 2nd Editions pg. 60 (2013)

William Penn

1. Keene, Cornell, O'Donnell "The Whig Vision Of Politics" Visions Of America 2nd Editions pg. 60 (2013)

Harrington believed that owning property gave individuals a permanent stake in society and also allowed men to be independent, voting for representatives without being manipulated or intimidated. (Visions of America pg. 54)

James Harrington
(Great Influence to William Penn)

1. Keene, Cornell, O'Donnell "The Whig Vision Of Politics" Visions Of America 2nd Editions pg. 60 (2013)

The Glorious Revolution

I respect what Mary II daughter of King James and William III did when they established the Glorious Revolution. Thankfully, word traveled back to the states where people began taking things out of the hands of the Puritan Orthodoxy rule of the established authority of Massachusetts.

They began establishing religious tolerance for all with clear cut boundaries of what would be permitted and what would not be tolerated. The protestant mindset moved local government that leaned more towards democracy or a free society while remaining under the authority of the British Empire. "Whig theory, put into place after the Glorious Revolution, put a premium on the ideal of civic virtue, placing the public good above personal interest.

To promote such virtue, one needed a society in which property ownership was widespread." I believe this would make for a happier nation where ever that were implemented.

1. Keene, Cornell, O'Donnell "The Whig Vision Of Politics" Visions Of America 2nd Editions
pg. 60 (2013)

Mary II

1. Keene, Cornell, O'Donnell "The Whig Vision Of Politics" Visions Of America 2nd Editions pg. 60 (2013)

William III

1. Keene, Cornell, O'Donnell "The Whig Vision Of Politics" Visions Of America 2nd Editions pg. 60 (2013)

Salem Witchcraft
An America Tragedy of Misunderstanding and Gross Injustices 1675

Supposedly, two Salem women and one Caribbean Indian slave named Tituba were accused of practicing witchcraft. Because of the Puritan practices of religion they went into hysteria in the community causing more accusations against others that may or may not have been true. This caused one innocent man to be stoned to death when he would not confess guilty or not guilty.

The Salem Witch Trials

1. Keene, Cornell, O'Donnell "The Whig Vision Of Politics" Visions Of America 2nd Editions pg. 60 (2013)

British Empire 1685

Thankfully, Mary II and William III new Glorious Revolution would put an end to these kind of atrocities against mankind by protecting basic rights that "excessive bails ought not to be required, nor excessive fines imposed, nor cruel and unusual punishment inflicted." This would have prevented the death of that innocent man.

However, had this happened after 1685 The Glorious Revolution when England unseated all the colonies authority and gave it back to the British Empire perhaps the man would not have been crushed by stoning?

1. Keene, Cornell, O'Donnell "The Whig Vision Of Politics" Visions Of America 2nd Editions pg. 60 (2013)

Glorious Revolution Medallion

1. Keene, Cornell, O'Donnell "The Whig Vision Of Politics" Visions Of America 2nd Editions pg. 60 (2013)

The Catholic Monarchy King James Strong Hand Over America: The Abolishment of the Representative Assemblies in the United States

Eventually, King Charles II died in 1685 and James II became England's first Catholic Monarch in 127 years. He became closely involved in the colonial affairs in New York and desired to consolidate the English colonies into larger administrative units.

He revoked and banished the charters of New York and New Jersey assigning them to New England. King James II tried to follow the Spanish agenda in New Spain. He wanted "a bold agenda to strengthen royal power at home."

He wanted to ally with Catholic France but his attempt to raise revenues through taxation. Parliament refused in Fall of 1688. British opponents Protestant Dutch Prince William of Orange and King James daughter overthrew the Monarchy and brought about the Glorious Revolution.

1. Keene, Cornell, O'Donnell "The Whig Vision Of Politics" Visions Of America 2nd Editions pg. 60 (2013)

King James II Monarchy

1. Keene, Cornell, O'Donnell "The Whig Vision Of
Politics" Visions Of America 2nd Editions
pg. 60 (2013)

The Mayflower Compact 1620

In the name of God, Amen. We whose names are under-written, the loyal subjects of our dread sovereign Lord, King James, by the grace of God, of Great Britain, France, and Ireland King, Defender of Faith, etc. Having undertaken, for the glory of God, and advancement of the Christian faith, and honor of our King and Country, a voyage to plant the first colony in the northern parts of Virginia, do by these presents solemnly and mutually, in the presence of God, and one of another, covenant and combine our selves together into a civil body politic, for our furtherance of the ends aforesaid; and by virtue hereof to enact, constitute, ordinances, acts, constitutions, and offices, from time to time, as shall be thought most meet and convenient for the general good of the Colony, unto which we promise all due submission and obedience. In witness whereof we have hereunder subscribed our names at Cape Cod, the eleventh of November, in the year of the reign of our sovereign lord, King James, of England, France, and Ireland, the eighteenth, and of Scotland the fifty-fourth. Anna Dom. 1620

1. Keene, Cornell, O'Donnell "The Whig Vision Of Politics" Visions Of America 2nd Editions pg. 60 (2013)

John Carver	William Bradford
William Brewster	Isaac Allerton
John Alden	Samuel Fuller
William Mullins	William White
John Craxton	John Billington
John Howland	Steven Hopkins
John Tilly	Francis Cook
Thomas Tinker	John Rigdale
John Turner	Francis Eaton
Digery Priest	Thomas Williams
Edmond Margeson	Peter Brown
Richard Clark	Richard Gardiner
Thomas English	Edward Doten
John Goodman	George Soule

1. Keene, Cornell, O'Donnell "The Whig Vision Of Politics" Visions Of America 2nd Editions pg. 60 (2013)

1. Keene, Cornell, O'Donnell "The Whig Vision Of Politics" Visions Of America 2nd Editions pg. 60 (2013)

www.ingramcontent.com/pod-product-compliance
Lightning Source LLC
Chambersburg PA
CBHW050850290526
45792CB00002B/604